Original title:
Purpose: Lost and Found in Translation

Copyright © 2025 Creative Arts Management OÜ
All rights reserved.

Author: Tobias Sterling
ISBN HARDBACK: 978-1-80566-093-4
ISBN PAPERBACK: 978-1-80566-388-1

Voices Across the Void

In the echo of a sneeze, they hear a laugh,
An awkward dance, a baffling half.
A cat that meows but speaks like a king,
And alas, the dog thinks it's a funny thing.

Lost in translation, they shake their heads,
A jumbled chorus of witty threads.
When asking for soup, they get a shoe,
Delightful chaos in a world so askew.

A mime shouts loudly, no sound in sight,
While a parrot squawks in the dead of night.
They wave a banner that reads 'Hello',
But it means 'Goodbye' in sunshine's glow.

Yet through the muddle, they find a spark,
A gleeful jest in the afterdark.
Though words may falter, smiles stay true,
In a world of mixed signals, joy breaks through.

Mismatched Rhythms

Bouncing beats on a broken drum,
A silent party; oh, how they come!
They clink their glasses to symbolize cheer,
But they toast to the cat that just can't steer.

Funky dance moves with two left feet,
A synchronization of the craziest beat.
They giggle and sway like boats in the sea,
As the yogurt spills, 'That's not supposed to be!'

A hula hoop tangled with bits of yarn,
And someone's wearing a bright green barn.
Running in circles, they dance with glee,
Caught in a rhythm that's simply not free.

Yet amidst the flailing, a joy comes through,
As laughter erupts like a wild zoo.
In mismatched beats, they find a song,
In off-key moments, they all belong.

Unearthed Realizations

Digging deep for treasures rare,
They find a sock, and perhaps a bear.
A fortune cookie whispers a riddle,
Is it a sign, or just a odd middle?

The map leads to a place quite sweet,
But ends at a rock, a funny retreat.
Where wisdom's buried beneath old fries,
Surprises pop up like ice cream pies.

In lessons learned, they breathe in bold,
Like a fancy jacket of threadbare gold.
Each wrong turn in this absurd race,
Turns frowns upside down with laughter in place.

Though the findings are odd and slightly bizarre,
They treasure the journey, oh, near and far.
In quirky insights, happiness thrives,
For the real gems are the laughs in our lives.

The Sound of Miscommunication

They ask for a pizza and get a fish,
Oh, the irony of a wild wish!
The waiter nods, but who can tell,
Is that a yes, or just a crinkle of hell?

Words twist in the air like balloon art,
A conversation that falls apart.
'Let's meet at dawn!' someone will call,
But it's dusk in the end, they all stall.

A laugh is mistaken for a loud cheer,
And whispering secrets brings folks near.
They fumble with phrases like juggling pies,
While all they wanted was a pie that flies.

Yet through the garble, they find a beat,
Laughter and smiles in a simple retreat.
In sounds of chaos, the joy can be found,
As they dance in the clash, all safe and sound.

Lost in the Nuance

I asked a chef for a spicy fix,
He handed me pickles and a box of tricks.
The menu's code was a riddle wrapped tight,
Now I'm craving ice cream at midnight's light.

Between his chuckles and my blank stare,
A dance of words lost in the air.
Like socks in the laundry, they tumbled around,
Now I just wonder what flavors I found.

Reflections of a Broken Compass

A compass spun like a cartoon bee,
Pointing me south while I longed for tea.
I followed the map, but oh what a scene,
Found myself lost in a circus routine.

With lions and jugglers and bright-colored lights,
I searched for directions in endless nights.
The stars were giggling, the moon gave a wink,
I laughed so hard, I forgot how to think.

Searching for the Unseen

With binoculars aimed at a field of green,
I searched for the unseen, like a quirky machine.
Instead of gold, I found an upside-down cat,
Wearing a top hat and looking quite fat.

It danced and it pranced, a sight to behold,
With tales of its travels, all wild and bold.
As I scribbled notes on the back of my hand,
I realized I was just part of its band.

The Distance of Dialogue

Two squirrels were chatting atop a tall tree,
And I wondered what grand thoughts would be.
Their tails waved like flags in a nutty parade,
While I sat on the ground, bewildered, dismayed.

They spoke of acorns and weather's new trends,
While I translated their chatter to my furry friends.
But between their wise tales and my blunders that day,
I concluded that squirrels may speak in ballet.

The Lost Art of Listening

In a world of loud chatter,
The mute cat's got the floor.
With heads in the screens,
Do we even know what's in store?

My friend talks about fish,
While I nod like a pro.
He thinks I'm all in,
But I'm just a forgetful show.

Wireless and clueless,
We lose what we meant to share.
Typing out 'LOL',
To a joke that's rare!

Perhaps it's time we trade,
Our screens for a laugh.
For listening's an art,
Not a digital gaffe!

Glimmers in the Dark

In the chaos of night,
A glow worm's throwing a rave.
Dancing to the silence,
While the owls mock and bray.

I starlit my way through,
But tripped on a large root.
The moon, it giggled slyly,
As I started to scoot.

Sparks fly from my ideas,
Like fireflies on a spree.
In shadows they flutter,
But really, who needs to see?

So here's to dim brilliance,
In the dark we'll ignite.
With flickers of laughter,
Let's make chaos a delight!

The Canvas of Tomorrow

With colors yet to blend,
I paint the dawn of fate.
Splashes of odd choices,
Like socks that don't quite mate.

The brushes are confused,
Should I use green or pink?
Art is just like life,
You never know what to think!

Each stroke tells a story,
Of chaos, joy, and cheer.
A masterpiece of mishaps,
That becomes my souvenir.

Let's grab our silliness,
And smear it on the wall.
In this wild wonderland,
Let's paint beyond the call!

Embracing the Unknown

I wake up, stretch my arms,
And yell, 'What's new today?'
The unknown winks back sweetly,
In a mysterious, quirky way.

What if I wear mismatched shoes?
Or try a brand-new dance?
Life's better being silly,
Grab every wacky chance!

I order cereal for dinner,
Mix it with hot sauce.
Taste testing life's options,
Oh dear, what a toss!

So here's to splashing boldly,
In puddles of the unreal.
For in every odd journey,
Lies the charm of the surreal!

The Echoes of Why

In the land of lost intentions,
A chicken crossed for a reason,
But the joke flopped hard, you see,
Now it's just a lunch-dilemma season.

Why do we chase after rhymes?
Like socks that vanish at spin cycles,
Searching for meaning in silly chimes,
While laughter sneaks and tickles.

What's the deal with those missed cues?
Like ordering soup with a fork,
Life's comic strips offer reviews,
As the punchline shuffles and corks.

In the maze of thoughts, I spin around,
Dodging pitfalls of profound despair,
Yet amidst chaos, giggles abound,
Finding joy in the antics we share.

Rediscovering the Unseen

In search of what we cannot touch,
I found a sock and a lost shoe,
Somebody's puzzle is way too much,
As I smile at what's askew.

What's cooking in the mind's muddle?
Like cats that play in the fog,
Every riddle is a silly cuddle,
Wagging tails turn into dialogue.

Once, I thought I lost my way,
But a squirrel showed me the route,
Dancing 'round without dismay,
Chasing dreams in a fruitless pursuit.

We gather treasures in odd places,
Like leftovers hoping for a friend,
While laughter paints our funny faces,
With each hiccup, we pretend.

Gleaning Truth from Mist

In a foggy town where no one sees,
A baker swears he bakes with ease.
But as he twists the dough with flair,
He sneezes flour into the air.

The cats all gather, cups on heads,
Declaring bread is best in beds.
But crumbs fall down like disco lights,
As neighbors fight with pastry bites.

The Lost Melodies

A trumpet played without a sound,
A squirrel danced, just spinning 'round.
The trees all laughed, their leaves a-flutter,
While bees disputed how to stutter.

A frog croaked high, then low with glee,
The crowd all cheered, 'What could it be?'
Yet when he leapt to join the song,
He missed the beat and fell quite wrong.

Echoes of a Silent Song

A melody that lost its beat,
Was found when ants marched down the street.
With tiny bows and strings so small,
They played a tune that charmed us all.

But as they danced on candy crumbs,
They slipped and tripped, with frantic blunders.
Each note became a silly fall,
Resounding laughter, after all!

The Journey Homeward

A snail decided to pack its shell,
For a trip that it knew too well.
It left a trail of lettuce greens,
And found a door where none had been.

But every time it tried to roam,
It picked a path that led to home.
The other creatures rolled their eyes,
As the snail claimed it held the prize!

Chasing Echoes

I chased a shadow, oh what a treat,
It danced and pranced on runaway feet.
I asked it for secrets, it just bounced back,
In whispers of giggles, it led me off track.

A friend joined the chase, with a net made of words,
Hoping to snare all those mischievous birds.
But they flapped away with a cheeky goodbye,
Leaving us laughing beneath the blue sky.

Translated Truths

I spoke in rhymes, you heard in beats,
We met in the middle, exchanged our seats.
Your smile was coding, my laugh was the key,
Together we laughed at our mystery.

We tried to connect with some cranky old slang,
But words turned to noodles, and then to a clang.
We giggled at meanings as we lost track,
Creating a symphony from the clatter and crack.

The Bridge of Interpretation

A bridge of confusion, that's where we meet,
With puns and mishaps, oh what a feat!
Our languages tangled like twisters in air,
Each word an acrobat, performing with flair.

I built a tall tower out of jumbled speech,
You threw in a pun that was quite out of reach.
We waved our flags of mismanaged delight,
As laughter rang out in the fading light.

Shattered Sentences

My sentences wobbled, they danced on the edge,
Like cats on a fence, making promises pledge.
You gathered the pieces, with grace and with flair,
As we turned scattered whispers into fresh air.

Each fragment a jigsaw, each laugh a bright spark,
In the chaos of nonsense, we found a new arc.
So let's toast to the jumble, the mix and the blend,
In the heart of confusion, we often transcend.

Shadows of Significance

In a world of chatter, I lose my vibe,
Hoping to find it, I scribble and scribe.
The cat thinks I'm nuts, it jumps on my lap,
While I ponder my words, like a sleepwalking map.

Did I mean to say apple, or perhaps a red hat?
As meanings slip by like a mischievous cat.
My thoughts do the cha-cha, they twirl and they spin,
In the shadows of meaning, where nonsense begins.

Unraveled Threads

I knitted a sentence, it's full of great flair,
But the yarn got tangled, now I've lost my hair.
A tangled-up sweater of phrases abound,
With labels that read 'lost', yet still make a sound.

The author within me is rolling in glee,
As I trip over puns, just like on my feet.
So I wade through the phrases like a diet of pies,
As threads unravel into colorful skies.

The Language of Unspoken Dreams

A whisper of wishes hides under my bed,
They giggle and dance, but refuse to be said.
They play peek-a-boo while I search for my pen,
To capture their secrets and start once again.

A dream dressed in purple, with shoes made of cheese,
Ponders aloud if it's too late to tease.
Oh, what a riddle! As they bounce off the wall,
The language of dreams is a curious call.

When Words Wander

Words on a journey, they stroll without care,
They take silly paths like they've lost their fare.
I called out to one, it turned with a grin,
Said, 'I'm simply exploring, won't you join in?'

With laughter we tumble, both lost and bemused,
Understanding together no longer confused.
When words start to wander, it's quite a delight,
In the wild wild west of the verbal moonlight.

Chronicles of the Unlived

In a world where dreams take flight,
The cat learns to dance late at night.
With socks on its paws, what a sight,
A party without any invite.

Old man Joe with a hat too wide,
Wonders where his lost socks reside.
Tangled tales of laundry pride,
Meanwhile, his goldfish laughs inside.

A toaster stubbed its little toe,
It dreams of being a star in a show.
With bread toasting in full glow,
It sighs, 'I wish I could go pro!'

Each toy soldier on the floor,
Debates their purpose, always more.
With marbles rolling, what a chore,
They scheme to find the exit door.

Reflections from the Edge

In a mirror where ducks wear hats,
A fish recites Shakespeare to cats.
It looks puzzled at all the spats,
As squirrels tape the world in spats.

A baker dreams of a cake so tall,
Yet each layer starts to have a brawl.
Frosting flying, sugar in thrall,
They laugh when it begins to fall.

The vacuum cleaner hums a tune,
Wishing it were a raccoon.
Chasing crumbs by the light of the moon,
It spins in circles, a wacky balloon.

With socks in the dryer, it's a race,
A missing match, a sneaky disgrace.
Yet in the chaos, finds its place,
In laughter, wrapped in warm embrace.

The Language of Longing

A potato wishes on a star,
To be a chip and go so far.
Yet finds itself in a pantry jar,
With dreams of salsa, now bizarre.

A lost umbrella yearns for rain,
As seagulls taunt it with disdain.
It flaps around, feeling the pain,
Of being left alone in Spain.

A couch laments its aching springs,
While counting all the little things,
That never quite fit into rings,
As it daydreams of flying flings.

The clock ticks with a silly face,
Wishing to join the human race.
"Let me dance!" it begs with grace,
A timepiece yearning for its place.

Seasons of Discovery

When spring calls with flowers bright,
A snail dons shades, looking quite tight.
Its friends all scramble, taking flight,
While it just basks in pure delight.

Summer arrives with a burning sun,
And ice cream cones that start to run.
A penguin slips, thinks it's all in fun,
As beach balls bounce, the chaos spun.

Autumn whispers with leaves that fall,
As pumpkins plot their big food stall.
They giggle as they roll, enthralled,
Creating crafts for one and all.

Winter comes, and snowballs fly,
While mittens laugh until they cry.
The world spins on, oh me, oh my,
In each season's game, we're all the why.

Finding Clarity in Chaos

In the midst of a wild, busy street,
I lost my way, ran on my own feet.
A pigeon laughed, pecked at my shoe,
'Follow my lead, I'll show you what's true!'

Maps crumple up, directions go wrong,
A GPS voice sings an off-key song.
I chase my tail with a confused look,
But maybe it's fun—this chaos, my hook!

Juggling oranges while sipping on tea,
A circus act that's perfect for me.
Life's a comedy, a quirky parade—
With laughter as compass, I won't be afraid!

So here's to the moments, both zany and bright,
For lost in translation, I'm finding delight.
The chaos, it dances, and I am the clown,
In this whimsical world, I wear no frown.

Between the Lines

I read a book with pages that sigh,
The chapters seem to wave me goodbye.
Lost in metaphors, I trip on the prose,
Between the lines, a wild party grows!

Footnotes tap dance, foot loose and free,
While commas and periods sip on sweet tea.
Each stanza giggles, unruly and loud,
As punctuation throws a raucous crowd!

The author blinks; what's happened, dear friend?
My plot's all twisted, on that you can depend.
But if words can wiggle and waddle about,
Perhaps they'll lead me, I'll follow, no doubt!

So here I stand, between phrases and rhymes,
Dancing with meanings, ignoring all times.
In books and in laughter, I'll find my own way,
For every mishap adds joy to my day!

Signs in the Silence

In a quiet room where crickets do chirp,
I look for answers, but I just feel a burp.
Whispers of wisdom float up to the sky,
While the echoes just giggle and flutter on by.

The walls are all painted in shades of unclear,
With secrets a-stirring, like soda and beer.
A sign on the fridge says, 'Don't seek, just eat,'
While I ponder the journey with crumbs on my feet.

In the gaps of the noise, a message is shared,
It's less about worries, more about dared.
Life's silly riddles in silence unfold,
With laughter as currency, and boldness as gold.

So I'll pause in the quiet, not fret nor regret,
For in stillness I find out new things, you bet.
The signs in the silence can often be found,
Like hidden confetti spread all around!

The Journey of Intention

I packed my bags with a wiggly grin,
Intending to travel, let the mischief begin!
With snacks and a hat, I set off in style,
But tripped on my shoelace—ah, what a wild mile!

Maps made of jello, I pull from my sack,
Each step is a dance, with rhythm, no lack.
'To where?' asks the wind with a chuckle and mock,
I shrug my shoulders—I'm just on the clock!

Wanderlust twinkles in every bright star,
With intentions that giggle, I'll venture afar.
A compass that spins like a topsy-turvy ride,
Guided by laughter, my joy is my guide!

So come join the quest, with banana peels neat,
Let's make merry missteps, don't skip a beat.
For every intention leads to surprises,
In the book of adventure, each page just rises!

Between Words and Whispers

In a world of chatter, we sometimes trip,
Words dance around like they've had a sip.
A giggle escapes where silence holds tight,
Meaning gets lost in the wild, silly flight.

A wink and a nod, but what did you say?
Your nodding's confusing, or is it just play?
Lost in translation, we chuckle and squawk,
All we really want is a good belly talk.

So here's my message, in a wordy haze,
Forget what I said, let's just count the ways.
With each silly blunder, let's laugh till we fall,
In this raucous game, we don't know it all.

When whispers confound but the laughter's sincere,
We find joy in nonsense, a comedic frontier.
So let's spin our words, like a topsy-turvy jive,
In this landscape of talk, we magically thrive.

The Puzzle of Being

Life's a game of Scrabble with letters that hide,
Playing for keeps, but they can't decide.
A jumbled mess on a slippery board,
Each word we create, oddly overlorded.

Inserting exclamations, and what's that there?
Is it a bear or a chair, please beware!
Misplaced intentions and typos galore,
Who knew that life held so much to explore?

With pieces of laughter like puzzle-shaped clips,
We find hidden meanings in tongue-twisted quips.
Each giggle a token for wrong turns we take,
Let's raise a glass to the slips we all make!

So gather 'round friends, let's mix and confound,
In the jigsaw of life, absurdity's found.
Together we'll weave this delightful charade,
As we puzzle our way through the jokes we have made.

Reclaiming the Unspoken

In the shade of a tree, we whisper and grin,
Words unspoken feel like a cheeky sin.
A nudge and a wink, we share silly plots,
Beneath all the talk, there are giggles and knots.

What can't be said might cause some dismay,
But let's turn that frown into a laugh today!
With glances and grins, let's start our own show,
In humor we find what the heart wants to know.

We dance around sentences, a waltz of fun,
The awkwardness sparkles, together we run.
So let's take our silence and make it a roar,
With jokes in the air, who needs words anymore?

In moments of pause, let our laughter resound,
As we reclaim each whisper, lost but now found.
With smiles that echo in the air that's around,
We'll make the unspoken the loudest sound.

Colliding Realities

When worlds collide like two trains of thought,
You wonder if something important was caught.
In the fog of confusion, misunderstandings grow,
But let's make a comedy out of the show!

Ideas collide like mismatched socks,
Two left feet dancing on paradox rocks.
A chuckle erupts when we mess up the grind,
In this clumsy ballet, we embrace the blind.

So let's merge our tales, from planets so far,
Each story a strawberry, life's bizarre bazaar.
Finding the humor in what's meant to baffle,
With laughter as currency, let's start a raffle!

In laughing together, the spark is ignited,
When colliding realities leave us delighted.
So here's to the chaos, the joy, and the play,
With jest as our guide, we'll laugh through the day.

The Language of Shadows

In the corner, shadows play,
Mimicking my awful ballet.
Whispers turn to raucous cheer,
Even the dark thinks I'm a dear.

Ghosts of my past throw a rave,
Dancing to tunes only they gave.
I trip on memories like stones,
While they laugh in their hushed tones.

With each step, a wobble, a sway,
Even shadows hide their dismay.
Lost in a fog of mismatched roles,
As they roll their ghostly scrolls.

At dusk, we chuckle, we collide,
In mischief, they gently abide.
If this is my fate, I'll take it fine,
With shadows as my friends, I shine!

Pathways to the Unknown

I set out with maps that don't align,
Trekking paths where squirrels dine.
Directions were a jumbled brawl,
Lost in a maze with no wall.

Every turn's a riddle, a jest,
Finding treasures like old chest.
"Is that a sign?" I dubiously croon,
It's a raccoon in a bright balloon!

Maps crumple under my heavy weight,
Each wrong turn leads to a plate.
Pasta in places of potholes found,
I gorge on noodles, truly renowned!

A journey of chaos, laughs, and fun,
I chase a sunset, forget the run.
In this mix-up, I've struck gold,
Through confusion, adventure unfolds!

The Symphony of Silence

In the quiet, echoes cry out,
Frogs croak solos, no doubt.
Birds hold the notes, forget their lines,
Nature's orchestra, tangled vines.

Mice on strings, a tiny band,
Playing tunes on grains of sand.
Crickets break into a rap,
While owls just nod—they're in a nap.

Silence shimmies, twirling about,
A whimsical waltz, no need to shout.
But wait! A gust with a twisty fate,
Blows away the beat—oh wait, and wait!

Laughter rolls like thunderous waves,
In this silence, we're all fools, brave.
Spinning in circles, that's our stance,
Clapping to rhythms, plunging in dance!

In the Wake of Undone

I woke up from dreams all askew,
With socks on my hands and a heart that flew.
Breakfast was blissfully botched, it's true,
Eggs bounced like balls on a wild blue.

To-do lists dance on the kitchen wall,
Each crossed-off line holds a silly call.
Laundry sings out of tune, "Don't forget!"
It seems even chores have no regret!

Routine's a jester in a green hat,
Playing tricks like a giant cat.
I stumble on chaos I just can't outrun,
In the wake of the undone—oh, what fun!

Embracing the mishaps, giggles erupt,
Life's a circus; will I interrupt?
So here I twirl, with laughter my crown,
In this carnival, I won't back down!

Reflections in the Mist

In the fog, my thoughts do drift,
Ideas tangled, like a gift.
I seek a key beneath the stew,
But find instead a soggy shoe.

Words jumbled like a game of charades,
What I mean often just fades.
A taco was once called a pie,
Guess my brain is asking 'Why?'

Lost messages in teapot's steam,
I bid goodbye to every dream.
I send my socks to save the day,
Here's hoping they can show the way.

In the haze I wear a grin,
For silly thoughts may just begin.
I laugh at what I can't define,
Finding reason in the whine.

Fragments of Forgotten Tales

A story starts, yet goes awry,
With missing bits that pass me by.
The dragon shrunk, or was it me?
In jokes I find my fantasy.

Once I met a knight in jeans,
Who claimed to save the world from beans.
With missing pages filled with glee,
I ponder if they're lost, or free.

Pages torn from lore I knew,
Become a recipe for stew.
Forgotten legends left to broil,
In lost translations, I must toil.

So turn the tales into a dance,
Add in a tune, give it a chance.
Just laugh it off, let whimsy fly,
In fragments, joy will multiply.

Legacies of Echoed Sorrow

Echoes ring from walls so tall,
Of laughter lost in the old hall.
A ghostly sigh might fill the air,
While my lunch waits without a care.

Each heartbreak sings, but what's the tune?
A melody played on a cello spoon.
I mope while dancing on a peg,
Can mischief stem from a broken leg?

In whispered tones of shadowed past,
I seek a reason, but none will last.
I penned my woes on a napkin bright,
But the ink was gone by the morning light.

So here's to grief, the jester's pride,
In echoes vast, let joy collide.
For in this mess, we find our way,
And celebrate the prankster's play.

The Heart's Faded Archives

In dusty shelves my heart resides,
With crumpled love notes deep inside.
I squint to read the faded lines,
Of choices mingled with the times.

What's better, cheese or a moonlit dance?
In old romance, I took a chance.
But mixed up hearts can lead astray,
As I brew coffee for a 'yay'.

Captured moments in a jar,
Of giggles, hiccups, dreams bizarre.
Yet translations blurred, they slip away,
In laughter's grip, we might just sway.

So here we are, a mix of joy,
With goof-ups that none can destroy.
In archives blurred, we make our mark,
As silly sparks ignite the dark.

Notes from a Forgotten Voyage

On a ship made of soggy bread,
The captain forgot where to tread.
With maps drawn by cats, they sailed wide,
Chasing fish who could giggle and hide.

The compass spun like a dervish,
As seagulls perched with great glee and swish.
An octopus scribbled a note,
Offering tips on staying afloat.

Each wave spoke in riddles and jokes,
While jellyfish danced with bright pokes.
The crew tried to catch a sunbeam,
But found only socks in the stream.

A Tapestry Unwoven

Once I wove threads of bright cheer,
But the needle took off for a beer.
My loom giggled, 'Now isn't this nifty?'
As knots formed like pandas, all thrifty.

My grandmother's yarn whispered tales,
Of knitting with whales and sailing in gales.
But one stitch got tangled in fish nets,
And oh, the fabric of fate, it forgets!

I sought for patterns, but they were all lost,
In a salad of colors, at a very high cost.
So I pranced with thread on a trampoline,
Bouncing my way to a life unforeseen.

Enigmas of the Soul

If my soul had a voice, it would croon,
Of socks in the dryer, lost too soon.
It whispers in riddles, with chuckles galore,
As it tries to remember what it's searching for.

It dances like a squirrel with a hat,
While pondering 'Why did I eat that?'
A donut of wisdom, it tastes quite divine,
But the icing drips down like a wayward sign.

Philosophers claim they've all got it right,
While my soul plays hopscotch, dodging the light.
It juggles confusion with joyous intent,
Waiting for the punchline, oh what a mess!

Chasing Faded Horizons

On horizons where giggles gleam,
We raced with our thoughts, a merry team.
With binoculars made of cardboard and glue,
We spotted a penguin in bright yellow shoes.

Our dreams had a flair for the dramatic,
While our plans turned out quite problematic.
We chased the sunset on a fluffy cloud,
Until it turned grumpy and shouted out loud.

But laughter erupted like bubbles in air,
As we tripped over dreams that didn't quite care.
So here's to the journeys we think are profound,
In the silliness, joy truly is found!

Hidden Connections

In a world of signs and signals,
My coffee cup said 'Espresso!'
But the spoon just laughed and giggled,
'You're a latte confused, you know?'

I wore mismatched socks all week,
Each foot seeking its lost twin.
The dryer must be a black hole,
Swallowing pairs with a silly grin.

The cat chased shadows on the wall,
While I debated the meaning of life.
Was it in the chase or the fall?
Or just the joy of the playful strife?

I bought a book on self-discovery,
But it came in a foreign tongue.
Now my heart's lost in translation,
For a rom-com that's never been sung.

The Quest for Clarity

I searched for wisdom in haikus,
But they left me in a tangle.
The meanings were like duck costumes,
Confusing, yet worth a wrangle.

I read a sign that said, 'Keep Calm,'
But my coffee spilled on my shirt.
Did that mean I should breath or scream?
Or just embrace the very absurd?

The wise owl hooted from a tree,
As I scribbled my thoughts of yore.
But wisdom was busy sipping tea,
Leaving clues like a scavenger tour.

I tried to distract my restless mind,
With puzzles riddled in reverse.
Finding clarity in chaos, I dreamed,
A riddle wrapped in a quirky verse.

Unveiling the Invisible

I pondered on the air I breathe,
And it chuckled back with glee.
'You can't touch what you can't see,'
It whispered with a breeze so free.

The clouds dressed up in a tuxedo,
As they floated past the sun.
Is it a party or a showdown?
With raindrops ruling, just for fun?

I tried to catch a fleeting thought,
With butterfly nets and jars.
But all I caught was a tickle,
And they giggled across the stars.

My quest for depth felt like a dance,
With shadows leading the parade.
Each step a mystery, a chance,
To laugh at the plans I had laid.

In Search of What Remains

I lost my keys in the sofa once,
Thought they took a vacation.
The couch replied, 'A silent dunce,
You're just part of the frustration!'

The map was a jigsaw of dreams,
Leading nowhere but close to home.
Each corner turned held a silly scheme,
Where laughter was all I'd roam.

With every question, answers fled,
As if playing hide and seek.
We found them in a sandwich spread,
That spilled while I tried to speak.

So here I stand with crumbs of wisdom,
From crumbs that were once a feast.
In this delightful, absurd rhythm,
I found joy in every least.

The Art of Rediscovery

I searched for my glasses, where could they be?
They sat on my head, just foolish me.
With a map in my hands, I ventured so far,
Only to find I was lost in my car.

A recipe called for a pinch of despair,
But I added a laugh, so it turned into flair.
The kids in the yard played tag with delight,
While I tried to fold laundry—it took all my might.

Turns out the lost sock was grander than gold,
For it danced on the floor like a story retold.
Amidst my confusion, I stumbled, then found,
Life's funny little quirks that abound all around.

Unraveled threads of Meaning

In search of a meaning, I brewed up some tea,
It spilled like my thoughts, oh what a sight to see!
A cat on the windowsill stretched out with glee,
While I pondered the mysteries of when and of we.

A note pinned to my fridge said, 'Eat more dessert!'
So I baked up a cake to feel less like dirt.
But with one slice gone, my thoughts fell askew,
As the frosting giggled, and the sprinkles just flew.

My life is an enigma wrapped up in a dream,
Like losing a puzzle piece—nothing's as it seems.
Yet when I least expect it, the laughter will shine,
And I'll find my reflections blend sweetly with wine.

Beneath the Surface

I dived into thoughts buried under my bed,
Where dreams turned to dust, and excuses were fed.
A rubber duck bobbed in a sea made of clothes,
While whispers of sanity danced on my toes.

I surfed on a wave of half-baked ideas,
With a side of confusion and much too much cheese.
The toaster volunteered to help with my plight,
Yet burned all my toast in the middle of night.

Beneath all the chaos, a giggle took flight,
As I wrestled with laundry stuffed far out of sight.
So, here's to the mess of misplaced intentions,
Where humor unearths tiny, blissful inventions.

Refracted Light

A prism of trickery shines in my mind,
Where rainbows of nonsense and logic entwined.
I squint at the world, in mirrors I stare,
With laughter reflecting, it's light as a pair.

I tackled the laundry, a mountain of fluff,
And danced with the dust bunnies, oh what a tough!
They taught me their secrets, I giggled and spun,
As the dryer made music, my soul just had fun.

In the kaleidoscope whir of life's funny maze,
The echoes of laughter will always amaze.
So when shadows might linger and humor looks dim,
Remember the light—it's just waiting for him.

The Dance Between What Was and What Is

In shoes two sizes too small, we tread,
Trying to dance, but we trip instead.
The past winks back with a mischievous grin,
While we wear our future like an old, dusty skin.

We shuffle and slip on the floor of our fate,
Salsa with moments, both heavy and great.
With a laugh we collide, a slapstick affair,
Unraveling stories we sometimes don't share.

The music is loud, the steps are all wrong,
But together we bumble, where we both belong.
In sock puppets twirling, we find simple bliss,
The dance of our lives, a comedic twist.

So let's spin and twirl in this grand masquerade,
With costumes of memories that never quite fade.
Each misstep a treasure, we wiggle and bob,
In the dance of today, where we giggle and sob.

Shadows of Lost Intent

In the corner, a shadow, once full of dreams,
Now lost in translation, or so it seems.
Waving its hands like a confused mime,
Trying to tell us it's just out of time.

It whispers sweet nothings like a half-baked croon,
About worlds where we danced beneath a bright moon.
But we squint in the darkness, pretending to see,
The punchline of jokes that might never be free.

Paper boats float on a puddle of thought,
Each one a goodbye, to the ideas we've sought.
The compass is spinning, a lost little sprout,
While we map out our endings, forgetting the route.

But in giggles and chuckles, we find our way back,
To the goofy impressions of a comical track.
The humor in chaos, that's where it begins,
In shadows that laugh, where the fun never ends.

Threads of Identity

Stitching a quilt from threads long since frayed,
Each patch a story, a memory played.
"Just what did I mean?" I laugh with delight,
As I twist and I turn in this colorful plight.

Each thread tells a tale, some tangled and long,
Like socks that have vanished—where do they belong?
I knot them together with giggles and grace,
Embracing the quirks that we all must embrace.

If identity's fabric is goofy and bright,
Then I'll wear my patchwork with utmost delight.
A blend of confusion, like flavors combined,
In a stew of existence, we're all intertwined.

So let's twirl with our threads in a colorful spin,
And knit a new world where the laughter kicks in.
In the tapestry woven, we find what we seek,
A merry connection, a whimsical peek.

The Tides of Understanding

The ocean of knowledge, it ebbs and it flows,
With waves of confusion that come and that go.
We surf on the chaos, equipped with a smile,
Finding depths of meaning, both shallow and vile.

"Dude, did you hear?" a wave of a friend,
"Understanding's tricky, but do not pretend!"
As we paddle together, a curious bunch,
Riding the current with laughter to munch.

The beach is our canvas, we dig with our toes,
Making castles of insights, where nobody knows.
A guided tour of folly, all twists and turns,
Yet in every stumble, a bright spirit burns.

So let's dive in together and splash through the muck,
Finding joy in confusion, it's totally luck!
The tides will keep shifting, but we won't float away,
In the ocean of laughter, we'll dance and we'll play.

Echoes of Meaning

In a world where words spin round,
I'm just a clown, with no sound.
I meant to say, please pass the bread,
But instead, I asked for a horse instead.

I typed away, my fingers flew,
Sent a note, hope it gets through.
But auto-correct had other plans,
Now I'm dating fish and tin cans.

Lost in translation, what a feat,
I wanted pizza, got sushi to eat.
Mom called for help, said "I'm so spent,"
I replied, "You need more condiment!"

At the end of this silly race,
I laugh at my own tomato face.
Meaning sometimes turns into jest,
But oh, how I love this chaotic quest!

Fragments of the Heart

You sent a text that broke my heart,
Dedication strong, till you hit 'start'.
Said you were coming, but what a turn,
You showed up with pizza, I wanted to burn.

Each message, a puzzle, mixed in glee,
You told me you loved my cat, not me.
I tried to confess my feelings, oh dear,
But all that came out was 'I love your beer!'

Trying to connect, we weave and we twist,
But somehow we both leave our points in the mist.
I winked, you blinked, signals all crossed,
Can you say 'Oops!' with a side of lost?

So here's to the laughter in all that we share,
Misunderstood tales floating in air.
Together we dance, though words come undone,
In this circus, I find we still have our fun!

The Art of Misunderstanding

I called you an angel, it sounds so divine,
But you thought I meant you should really define.
You scribbled and laughed, said 'That's quite rare',
While I just sat dreaming, lost in your stare.

Metaphors tangled, words on the floor,
I wanted to hug, you wanted a roar.
Told you I'd travel, see sands of the sea,
You packed up your bags, took my cat with glee!

Conversations like puzzles, each piece amiss,
You hand me a cupcake while I ask for a kiss.
It's a comic ballet, our dialogue's dance,
Twists of confusion in every romance.

From laughter to blunders, we shift and we sway,
In this jumbled saga, come join me and play.
So raise a toast to the chaos, my friend,
In the art of misunderstanding, we'll never end!

Whispered Intentions

I whispered sweet nothings, oh what a start,
You thought I was asking for directions, dear heart.
I wanted romance, with candles aglow,
Instead got the GPS to Mississippiro.

You dreamed of great heights, I just wanted fries,
A burger, a shake, but you heard 'surprise!'
I brought you a flower, you brought me a book,
You read it aloud, after one funny look.

Each secret desire, a game of charades,
I waved my arms, thought we'd dance in parades.
You heard me say 'let's swim in the goo',
I said 'let's just swim' – much cleaner, it's true.

So here's to the giggles, the meanings that slide,
In this wacky world, let's take it in stride.
For whispered intentions can turn into cheer,
And every good story needs laughter, my dear!

Journeying through the In-between

In a land where socks go missing,
I search for dreams that slipped away.
With mismatched shoes and frayed ambitions,
I laugh at plans that went astray.

The GPS is lost, it seems,
Giving directions like a cranky cat.
I wander through my silly schemes,
Searching for that golden hat.

Each step feels like a silly dance,
Tripping over thoughts that roam.
I take a leap, a goofy prance,
And build a castle made of foam.

Yet through the chaos and the spree,
I find a glimmer, bright and bold.
In this in-between, I finally see,
Laughter's worth more than gold.

Sifting through Silent Histories

Old boxes filled with dusty yeasts,
Tell stories that nobody knows.
A loaf of bread with tiny beasts,
Crumbs of past, where nothing grows.

I sift through notes of ancient types,
Words that lost their way in flight.
My grandma's tales of longing pipes,
And now I'm just trying to get it right.

Each letter laughs, a quirky chap,
Winks and nods, a playful tease.
I can't quite grasp the hidden map,
But oh, it feels like a breeze!

At last, I ditch the weighty tome,
Embrace the whimsy in my head.
In every silent nook and dome,
Lies a chuckle for the fed.

The Words We Never Spoke

There sat a word on tiptoes shy,
Hiding behind a giggling grin.
It wanted to soar, to touch the sky,
But instead, it trips on a pin.

A phrase once bold now lost in time,
It fumbled through my muddled brain.
Structuring a poem—oh, what a crime!
Puns in layers, joy's the gain.

Twisted sentences, made me chuckle,
A thesaurus starts to frown,
Yet here I am, in a joyful struggle,
As meanings dance and swirl around.

The words may slip, but I'm not sore,
For laughter is the thread that binds.
In every gap, there's so much more,
As I play with these quirky finds.

Murmurs of Forgotten Intent

In secret corners, voices chatter,
Whispers of dreams we couldn't bet.
A plan to bake, it fell to splatter,
Now it's soup, and I'm upset.

Forgotten lists on napkins stained,
With doodles more than wise advice.
My hopes in chaos, sweetly chained,
Tickle my heart, they're so precise.

A half-formed joke, it lingers near,
Trying to find its punchline's grace.
Yet laughter comes, without a fear,
As we stumble through this mad race.

In every murmur, there's a tease,
A winking joke that makes me grin.
I find the joy in chaos, please,
For lost intent is where I've been.

Pathways Crafted in Shadows

I wandered down a path unseen,
With signs that said 'Eat Here, Not Green.'
A fork in the road, and I took a dive,
Only to find a waiter who's five.

The trees had whispers, the wind told jokes,
A squirrel gave me tips, as if he knows folks.
I slipped on a root, said 'that's just my luck,'
The shadows just laughed—my spirit they struck.

A lantern bug danced, lit up my route,
In shadows, they giggled, hey, that's not astute!
Yet still I traveled, a map upside-down,
Found treasure in laughter, not just a crown.

In shadows so deep, I found humor bright,
Discovery winked in the flickering light.
So I'll take the path, unmarked and absurd,
For in all the folly, my heart sings its word.

Secrets of the Unexpressed

There was a cat who plotted a scheme,
To catch a fish that spouted cream.
He practiced his pounce, but tripped on a shoe,
And landed in a puddle—oh, what a view!

The fish just chuckled, splashed with delight,
'You need more practice, maybe tonight?'
It swam in circles, a watery king,
While cat sat soggy, pondering spring.

He whispered to pigeons, "What's in a word?"
They cooed back secrets, sometimes absurd.
A riddle, a ruckus, a pun in the air,
Unexpressed wishes, with flair and a scare!

Beneath all the layers, the laughter would swell,
In a world of antics, who can truly tell?
With secrets all jumbled, they twirled like confetti,
For in every mishap, the humor was ready.

The Horizon of What Could Be

A sandwich in hand, dreams stacked high,
I reached for the stars, but missed the pie.
With crumbs on my face, a grin on my chin,
Imagining worlds, where logic won't win.

A trampoline beckoned, 'Bounce into air!'
So I leaped with great fervor, caught only despair.
For the sky was just blue, and I went whoosh!
Landed on daisies, still seeking my swoosh.

With a jellybean map, I strolled down the lane,
Dreams filled with candy, bananas, and rain.
"Where's the horizon?" I asked a wise frog,
He blinked twice and croaked, "You're stuck in a fog!"

Through giggles and blunders, I sprinted with glee,
To horizons of laughter, where wildflowers spree.
In a journey unending, with whimsy so free,
Life's bigger than sandwiches—come bounce with me!

Threads of Reclamation

In a world stitched together with yarn that won't fray,
Saw a sock with a story, lost in the fray.
It moaned of a match that went sadly awry,
For each step it took, left a sock-whoopee cry.

The cozy knit whispers in colors so bright,
Knick-knacks from chaos, heartwarming sight.
A tapestry spun of flops and of fumbles,
Where laughter is woven through all of our tumbles.

"Reclaiming my time," said the thread with a wink,
As they danced with the buttons, swaying to think.
A quilt full of joy, mischief, and cheer,
Reminds me that losses can turn into beer!

So here's to the wrinkles, each twist and each bend,
For life is a knitting that won't surely end.
In threads of reclamation, we find our own song,
With humor as fabric, we cannot go wrong!

The Bridge Between

Two minds collide in playful jest,
Words slip and slide, who knows best?
Pointing and laughing, a finger here,
Translation's a game, let's all cheer!

Connect the dots, or maybe not,
Lost in meanings, oh what a plot!
A bridge of giggles, don't take it hard,
Just sip the tea and play the bard.

Chasing the facts like a dog with a ball,
Running in circles, we trip and fall.
A wink, a nod, and whoosh—oops!
In this funny dance, we're all just flukes.

So here's to the charm of mixed-up tales,
Where nothing makes sense but laughter prevails.
Let's toast to the bridge we all may cross,
In this silly world, there's never a loss!

Silent Conversations

Whispers and giggles in a crowded room,
I nod my head, what's causing the gloom?
Eyes wide open, I mimic a grin,
In this quiet chat, let the fun begin!

Gestures abound like a dance on cue,
What does it mean? I haven't a clue.
You wink and I smile, it's all quite absurd,
A secret language, not a spoken word.

You raise an eyebrow, I smirk in reply,
Each subtle movement, a question on high.
In this mute exchange, my brain starts to fry,
Yet laughter erupts, oh me, oh my!

Silent pursuits that twist and that turn,
In the realm of the quiet, let mischief churn.
With each silent chuckle, our bond starts to grow,
In this strange, crazy talk, just enjoy the flow!

Notes of the Untold

Jotted down thoughts on a napkin with flair,
Doodles and scribbles, a whimsical affair.
Partial stories lost in a haze,
Each line a chuckle, a puzzling maze.

Lost in translation, the letters collide,
What's meant to be clear takes a fun ride.
I read my notes, laughter starts to swell,
The hidden meanings aren't hard to tell.

Grappling with phrases, like juggling pies,
Messy concoctions, all laughter-filled sighs.
Each untold note can spark a delight,
In the chaos of meaning, we find our light.

So here's to the scribbles of life's crazy song,
Where misprints and giggles go hand in hand strong.
In this muddled dance of forgotten lore,
Let's turn the page, and humor's encore!

Ghosts of Ambition

Chasing dreams like a cat with a string,
Tangled in hopes that make our hearts sing.
The ghosts of ambition float by with a grin,
In spooky pursuits, let the fun begin!

Boo! What was that? Oh, just an idea,
Whispering softly, oh dear, oh dear!
In the attic of dreams, shadows make plans,
Between fits of laughter and five-second stands.

Mistakes wobble by in a spectral dance,
Misguided moments and cheeky romance.
We laugh at their folly, the ghosts shake their chains,
In this haunted ambition, we all share the gains.

So here's to the mischief of chasing the great,
Embracing the silly at each twist of fate.
Let's raise a glass to the plans that we find,
With laughter in hand, we're never maligned!

Maps of the Unseen

In a world full of signs, I took a wrong turn,
My GPS laughed, said, 'You have much to learn!'
With every new corner, confusion would grow,
But hey, it's the journey, not where you go!

I tripped on a thought, it danced on my shoe,
It whispered sweet secrets, all shiny and new.
A treasure map upside down in my hand,
Leading me places I don't understand!

I found an odd rock that looked just like pie,
The squirrels all sang, and I wondered why.
I followed a trail marked 'beware of the duck',
And stumbled on breadcrumbs—what a fine luck!

So here's to the paths that go nowhere fast,
Where laughter is plenty and dull moments are cast.
For maps of the unseen take us far and wide,
And lead us to giggles, with chaos as our guide.

Shattered Reflections

In the mirror, I peep, see my hair in a mess,
The reflection just grins, like it's playing a jest.
'What's happened to you?' I ask with a pout,
It winks and replies, 'It's all turned inside out!'

I wore mismatched socks, a potato for luck,
With all of my plans just sitting in muck.
But each laugh shared rolled like bubbles in air,
As if my old worries were nothing to wear.

Puddles laugh loud when I jog through the rain,
Splashing my dreams, it's a jubilant pain.
'Your life's like a puzzle,' the reflections did tease,
'But who put it together? It's all just a breeze!'

So I'll dance with the shards of my colorful face,
Collecting the echoes that litter this place.
For shattered reflections show pieces of glee,
And life's silly fragments are all part of me.

Clarity Amidst the Chaos

In the chaos of clowns, I found a giraffe,
Wearing a tie, and a peculiar laugh.
He pointed his neck straight toward the bright moon,
Saying, 'Join in the fun, don't leave it too soon!'

While juggling my thoughts, I slipped on a line,
Made friends with a rubber band, feeling just fine.
With each new distraction, I learned to embrace,
The madness that swirled like a dance in my face.

So with gumdrops for eyes and sprinkles for teeth,
I fashioned a tune, good vibrations beneath.
Clarity's a joke! It's a ride with a twist,
And each silly moment's too good to resist!

In the carnival lights where confusion is king,
I've searched for my sanity, found my own fling.
For clarity's nothing but laughter unbound,
And chaos is simply the best kind of sound.

Fragments of a Silent Journey

With shoes full of jelly, I wandered away,
Through echoes of whispers that had much to say.
Each step was a riddle, with giggles in tow,
As nonsense collected like snow in a row.

The map was a cupcake, the path made of cheese,
I met a wise turtle who giggled with ease.
He offered some wisdom packed in a box,
Said, 'Keep light in your heart, avoid all the rocks!'

With fragments of laughter that glittered the ground,
I danced with my dreams in a treasure profound.
Though silence would whisper in murmurs so bright,
Each joke on my journey felt perfectly right.

In the end, all the pieces of joy that I'd found,
Were scattered like bubbles, all floating around.
So here's to the journey, the jokes we have spun,
With silence as music, we're never quite done!

Fleeting Moments of Clarity

In the midst of chaos we stand,
Searching for meaning, not quite planned.
A squirrel's dance catches our eye,
And suddenly, we're questioning why.

Coffee spills on the table bright,
Turns our worries into a sight.
Do we laugh or do we frown?
Maybe a donut will calm us down.

Amidst the jargon, a word takes flight,
Escaping the jargon, feeling just right.
Was that wisdom or just a pun?
We'll ponder it over, fun yet done.

And in these moments, humor's our guide,
Navigating the bumpy ride.
We giggle at life, pretend we know,
It's a wacky ride – just go with the flow.

Hues of Dissonance

The colors clash like socks in a drawer,
Red with pink? Who could ask for more?
We paint our dreams with shades askew,
Wondering what on earth to do.

Maybe that blue is really green,
Or is it chartreuse? What does it mean?
Sometimes hues blend, sometimes they fight,
Learning the art of wrong and right.

Confusions twirl in a pie chart's dance,
In miscommunication, we take a chance.
Paint splatters tell stories so loud,
That we smile amidst the colorful crowd.

Through laughter and chaos, colors collide,
Creating a masterpiece where we reside.
It's a canvas of life, oh what a tease,
In all this dissonance, we find our ease.

Crossroads of Silence

At the intersection of thought and doubt,
Where silence reigns, we start to shout.
Do we take left? Or the road that's right?
We flip a coin, hope for insight.

Birds chirp loudly, yet no one hears,
While we contemplate our hopes and fears.
"Mmm, maybe pizza should lead the way,"
Or perhaps a nap? What do you say?

Amidst the stillness, we laugh at fate,
As life's little twists seem to abate.
We'll dance on the lines of daydreams gray,
Finding our voices in the silliness of play.

In quirky quietude, ideas entwine,
A light-hearted journey, oh how divine!
Though silence is loud, it's filled with sound,
In the stillness of laughter, wisdom is found.

The Path Yet Untaken

With boots untied, we stride ahead,
To places unknown, where dreams are spread.
A map in hand, or maybe not,
We'll wander the paths that life forgot.

Every twist, a giggle, every turn, a cheer,
Finding joy in the absurd—oh dear!
Unexpected detours to explore and find,
A treasure chest filled with peace of mind.

Footprints fade, and yet we roam,
Collecting strange stories that feel like home.
In the circus of choices, we laugh, we play,
Taking chances, come what may.

So here's to the routes we haven't yet tried,
With whimsy in heart, and stars as our guide.
For in every journey, humor's the key,
Unlocking the doors to who we can be.

Etchings of Identity

A crab walked sideways down the lane,
It sang a song about its pain.
With claws that clacked and eyes that gleamed,
It doubted if its heart was deemed.

A fish in boots tried to take a stroll,
Complained about its lack of a role.
In puddles deep, it tried to swim,
Yet found no talent, just a whim.

An elephant lost in a hat parade,
Said, "I wish I could just fade!"
But every time it tried to hide,
It trumpeted, and all eyes pried.

A cat once thought it could play the role,
Of lion king in a tiny shoal.
But in a box, it found its throne,
Claiming all naps as its own.

The Veil of Understanding

A parrot squawked, 'I know it all!'
While missing out on the cannonball.
With feathers bright yet eyes so dim,
It'd give advice, then lose its whim.

A snail debated, fast or slow,
Claiming speed's just fashion show.
Yet with a trail that stretched a mile,
It smiled broad with every trial.

A hamster wrote a big old book,
On how to eat without a cook.
But every chapter was a joke,
The punchline slipped, and laughter broke.

A frog in shades croaked out a tune,
Ignoring shades of silver moon.
It leapt from dreams without a sound,
A comedy of errors crowned.

Tales of Wandering Hearts

A wayward sock danced with delight,
Frolicking in the laundry night.
It searched for mates, a perfect match,
Yet pairs were lost, just a scratch.

A wanderer lost in a pickle jar,
Said, "Do I travel near or far?"
The brine was thick, the journey long,
But in the end, a vinegar song.

A rubber duck took a grand old trip,
Sailing with pirates on a sinking ship.
But every wave brought hiccups loud,
As it realized it wished to crowd.

A pizza slice looked for its pie,
Dreaming of cheese in the sky.
Each topping told tales of where it's been,
But still, it wondered, when's the cheese win?

Lost in the Ambiguity

A pencil thought it wrote a letter,
But scribbled lines just made it fetter.
With erasers busily at work,
It pondered hard to avoid the quirk.

A jelly bean wished it could fly,
But bounced around, oh my, oh my!
It sought a path to sugary lands,
Where every flavor had its fans.

A couch potato tried to sprint,
But soon became a comfy hint.
It lounged with chips, proclaimed it proud,
'Hey, keep the party, I'll remain cloud!'

A fortune cookie cracked its shell,
Promising wonders none could tell.
But instead of wisdom, just a "meh,"
It laughed at life, and sipped some tea.

www.ingramcontent.com/pod-product-compliance
Lightning Source LLC
Chambersburg PA
CBHW072145200426
43209CB00051B/494